KU-054-785

Contents

Introduction

Children in the Early Years Foundation Stage (EYFS) are developing rapidly in every way. Through play, children are exploring and discovering their world; developing the ability to share and interact with others; learning how to communicate with adults and other children. During the EYFS we expect children to become:

- skilful communicators – both listening and speaking;

- socially competent – able to cope with different situations and take turns;

- strong and healthy – well co-ordinated to cope with climbing, running and jumping and learning how to handle tools and small objects with confidence and control;

- familiar with early skills and concepts – knowing about size, shape, colours, numbers, rhythm and rhyme;

- explorers and discovers – curious about the world around them and confident to ask questions and get involved.

Children develop unevenly and many will have real strengths in certain areas. For example, some children love creating pictures and models in lots of different ways, and this ability may well stay with them into adulthood.

Others will be excellent communicators with a command of vocabulary that seems to be beyond their years.

Many people associate dyslexia mainly with school age children, and this is appropriate, because it is not possible to make a reliable diagnosis until a child is around the age of seven or eight. There can be many reasons for developmental delay. The young child who attempts to write the first letter of their name, but repeatedly does it backwards, need not give cause for concern. It is only when this kind of difficulty persists beyond the EYFS and is accompanied by other features that a diagnosis can be made; after careful records have been kept on the child's progress and this has led to the formal involvement of other professionals. The role of the Early Years Practitioner is to meet the individual needs of all children. This includes their physical development and their emerging skills in communication, literacy and numeracy. The aim of this book is not to trigger premature diagnosis but to give ideas of how to support children's development in the above areas by understanding that children learn in different ways.

Children who are experiencing difficulties with physical co-ordination, or remembering rhymes or instructions, do not necessarily have the early signs of dyslexia, but the strategies and ideas in this book can still be used to help and support them in their learning.

Who is this book for?

This book is for all practitioners working with young children, who want to understand, value and support all the children in their setting. Many of the practical ideas and suggestions are relevant for all children, not just those with additional needs.

This book will:

Inform you by:

- explaining what dyslexia is all about;

- introducing the idea of different learning styles that will help you support children's learning;

- emphasising that children who are eventually diagnosed as having dyslexia can have unusual skills in other areas;

- reporting on how it feels to cope with dyslexia, including feelings of low self-esteem.

- describing some of the early signs that you might see and explaining how you address these with regard to the SEN Code of Practice;

- giving details of other professionals and agencies who can become involved with children who are experiencing difficulties;

Inform you by:

- giving practical, tried and tested ideas and strategies across the six areas of learning, including multi-sensory approaches;

- providing reassurance that it is not appropriate to make or suggest a diagnosis at this stage;

- giving examples of IEP targets for children on Early Years Action support;

- discussing best practice when working with parents;

- explaining good practice for record keeping and tracking progress, with examples;

- showing how you can help children to develop their strengths.

Inspire you by:

- giving insight into the parents perspective;
- suggesting loads of easy activity ideas;
- describing good ideas for a smooth start tolearning in your setting.

Make you think by asking:

- how might it feel to have difficulties interpreting print and symbols?
- what's it like to feel different?
- what's it like to parent a child with special needs?
- how can you help other children understand the problems?

Make you ask yourself some hard questions such as:

- how can I make real connections with this child?
- what do I need to do for this child to enable them to make the most of the Early Years Foundation Stage?
- how can I help children understand, value and support others in my setting?

What is Dyslexia?

The word **'dyslexia'** comes from the Greek and means 'difficulty with words'. Researchers have established that people with dyslexia process information differently from those who do not have dyslexia. People with dyslexia often have **distinctive talents** as well as **typical clusters of difficulties**.

Around 4% of the population is severely dyslexic. A further 6% have mild to moderate problems. Dyslexia occurs in people from all backgrounds and of all abilities, from people who cannot read to those with university degrees. People with dyslexia, of all ages, can learn effectively but often need a different approach. Dyslexia is a puzzling mix of both difficulties and strengths which vary in degree and type from person to person.

Two of the main areas of difficulty usually associated with dyslexia are **slow phonological development and inefficient short-term memory:**

- Phonological development includes the skills of distinguishing and manipulating sounds within words, detecting and producing rhyme. Phonological development is closely linked to reading development.

- An efficient short-term memory is essential to learning at any age. Information must be held within the short-term memory long enough for the brain to transfer it to the long-term memory.

Supporting ideas

Under each of the six areas of learning in the Foundation Stage (pages 23-38) there are lots of suggestions, using everyday resources, that are planned specifically for children with early signs of dyslexia. All the ideas provide opportunities for small step learning, repetition and reinforcement. They are written to take careful account of the implications of emerging dyslexia on individual children's learning.

Some definitions of dyslexia

1. Dyslexia has been estimated to occur in 4% of the UK population, and 10% show some of the symptoms of dyslexia. It has been defined by the British Dyslexia Association as "a combination of abilities and difficulties that affect the learning process in one or more of reading, spelling, writing. Accompanying weaknesses may be identified in areas of speed of processing, short-term memory, sequencing and organisation, auditory and/or visual perception, spoken language and motor skills. It is particularly related to mastering and using written language, which may include alphabetic, numeric and musical notation."

2. Dyslexia is also known as Reading Disorder. The symptoms of dyslexia are measured by reading achievement, i.e., reading accuracy, speed or comprehension as measured by standardized tests, that falls substantially below that expected, given the individual's chronological age, measured intelligence, and age appropriate education (DSM-IV Dyslexia 1994). Dyslexia symptoms can show up for a variety of reasons. http://www.ldhope.com/dyslexia.htm

3. Dyslexia. A disorder where things are done or read backwards. For example, a 'd' and a 'b' might be confused. http://www.macalester.edu/psychology/whathap/UBNRP/synesthesia/terms.html

4. Dyslexia: An impairment of the ability to read. Early diagnosis and educational intervention are essential. http://chfs.ky.gov/dcbs/dpp/adoptionglossary.htm

5. Dyslexia is a complex learning difficulty which impacts on a learner's ability to read, write and count. http://www.health-forums.com/

6. Inability or difficulty in reading, including word-blindness and a tendency to reverse letters and words in reading and writing. http://www.michigan.gov/mcsc/0,1607,7-137-6002-61850--,00.html

7. Dyslexia is a specific type of learning difficulty where a person of normal intelligence has persistent and significant problems with reading, writing, spelling and, sometimes, mathematics and musical notation. The person may not have difficulties in other areas: many dyslexic people are extremely creative, think laterally and have excellent problem-solving skills. It may be helpful to think of dyslexia as an information processing difficulty. Dyslexia is a complex learning difficulty because of the number of characteristics associated with it, such as lack of phonological awareness, poor short-term memory or confusion about left and right, which vary from individual to individual. http://www.invisibledisabilitytraining.co.uk/Dyslexia.html

8. The Literacy Dictionary defines dyslexia as: A developmental reading disability, presumably congenital and perhaps hereditary, that may vary in degree from mild to severe. Note: Dyslexia, originally called word blindness, occurs in persons who have adequate vision, hearing, intelligence, and general language functioning . . .
[Source: Harris, T. & Hodges, R. (Eds.). (1995). The Literacy Dictionary. Newark, DE: International Reading Association.]
From Teacher's Guide by Sherrye Dee Garrett, Ed.D for 'Reading the Sky' A Breakfast Serials Story written by Avi and illustrated by Joan Sandin
http://www.usethenews.com/UTN%20guide%20samples/ReadingTheSkySAMPLE.pdf

9. "Dyslexia is one of several distinct learning disabilities. It is a specific language-based disorder of constitutional origin characterized by difficulty in single-word decoding, usually reflecting insufficient phonological processing. These difficulties in single-word decoding are often unexpected in relation to age and other cognitive and academic abilities; they are not the result of generalized developmental disability or sensory impairment. Dyslexia is manifested by variable difficulty with different forms of language, often including, in addition to, problems with reading, a conspicuous problem with acquiring proficiency in writing and spelling."
Working definition of dyslexia approved by the International Dyslexia Association Research committee, April 1994, in collaboration with individuals from the National Center for Learning Disabilities and the National Institutes of Child Health and Human Development USA.
http://www.txkisd.net/curriculum/Dyslexia.htm

10. Dyslexia is a syndrome in which a person's reading and/or writing ability is significantly lower than that which would be predicted by his or her general level of intelligence. People are diagnosed as dyslexic when their reading problems can not be explained by lack of intellectual ability, or by inadequate instruction, or by sensory problems such as poor eyesight. Because reading is a complex mental process, dyslexia has many potential causes. From a neurophysiological perspective, dyslexia can be diagnosed by close inspection of the morphology of the brain (usually upon autopsy). Dyslexia is also being associated with phonological difficulties, such as enunciation.
http://www.bambooweb.com/articles/D/y/Dyslexia.html

As you can see, there is a wide difference of opinion on the causes of dyslexia, but a great deal of agreement about its efffects!

Learning styles and multiple intelligences

Much has been written and researched about people having preferred learning styles. Dr Howard Gardner of Harvard University, in his book 'Frames of the mind', identified the fact that we have not just academic intelligence that can be measured with IQ tests, but seven different intelligences, or natural talents, which we have in different measures. Each intelligence carries equal importance if we are going to reach our full potential.

Linguistic Intelligence

The ability to write or talk well. As professionals working with children, we begin to wonder about signs of dyslexia when children who are really clever when they talk about things seem confused by the written word. We expect the two skills to go together.

Mathematical/Logical Intelligence

You can probably think of people who do not see themselves as highly intelligent but are sharp at dealing with numbers. Market traders and darts players might fall into this group. Engineers, scientists and accountants also excel in this type of intelligence.

Visual/Spatial Intelligence

The ability to visualise how things will look when they are finished, before they are even started. People with dyslexia often have exceptional skills in this area which makes them good at things like pottery, art and design. Richard Rogers, one of Britain's greatest modern architects is dyslexic. We all use this visual intelligence when we use our sense of direction or navigation. It has been discovered that some people with dyslexica have unique skills because of their ability to approach tasks in a different way from the rest of us.

Musical Intelligence

The ability to create or interpret music. People with dyslexia often benefit from the use of music and rhyme to learn, but this is something that all young children benefit from because of the power of multi-sensory learning techniques which help a child to 'fix' things in their brain. For young children, learning through music and chanting in groups has all sorts of benefits. Older children with dyslexia may still be relying on these techniques into their teens and this should be allowed for by their teachers.

Bodily/Physical Intelligence

People who are good with their hands are demonstrating their own form of intelligence which is often envied by the more academic amongst us. People with dyslexia can make very good builders because they can interpret the architect's plans really well. Sports people, athletes and dancers also have this intelligence in abundance.

Inter-personal Intelligence

The ability to be socially competent and a good communicator. This is a highly prized skill in our society, as we all enjoy the company of someone who makes others feel at ease because they are skilled at reading reactions and being sympathetic to other people's feelings. Children thrive in the company of teachers, parents and carers who have this intelligence.

Intra-personal Intelligence

Being in touch with your own behaviour and feelings. Some some people with dyslexia are overwhelmed by their difficulties when coping with the written word, a skill which we believe to be essential to do well in the western world. They feel out of step and wearied by the demands of a school day and may react by being withdrawn or by demonstrating challenging behaviour. Others can use this intelligence to set their own goals and use their successes and errors to guide them towards coping with the pressures. A good teacher or teaching assistant can help, and a supportive family is invaluable but the inner strength and this intelligence comes from the learner themselves.

Naturalist Intelligence

In later works Howard Gardner has identified one other intelligence which we would recognise immediately. This is the love of, and fascination with, the natural world from slugs and ants to dinosaurs and elephants. We all know children and adults who have this intelligence!

Emotional Intelligence

There has been much interest recently in the work of Daniel Goleman and his belief in the existence of Emotional Intelligence. This is 'the awareness of and ability to manage one's emotions in a healthy and productive manner.' We all need this and some of us have it in higher quantities than others. With help, children can increase their ability to use this intelligence and turn it into 'Emotional Literacy'. This is important because we cannot assume that all children know what an angry, happy, surprised or sad face looks like. We need to help children to learn to read the signs of emotion in others and in themselves. We speak of giving children verbal and non-verbal messages to show our approval or disapproval of their actions. Research shows that some groups of children, for example some children on the autistic spectrum and some boys, when responding to some female voices, fail to notice what we may think are obvious messages. This is often interpreted as being deliberately ignored! It is therefore important to work on emotional literacy with all children from an early age.

Thinking skills

Most professionals working in education also believe that the encouragement and development of thinking skills are vital in learning for children of all ages, including those who have special needs.

Such skills can be nurtured from a very young age:

- Problem solving activities can have a beneficial effect on learning, and should be used with children of all ages.

- The use of effective and open ended questioning is a skill that all adults who work with children can learn in order to help them to extend problem solving skills and to be curious about the world in which they live.

- Collaborative and group activities can be planned, even for very young children, to help them with sequencing, analysing and decision making. They should be encouraged to discuss their thinking as they work together.

- A good practitioner will soon learn the value of observing these activities – recording where necessary how the group interact, who is a natural leader and who finds such interactions difficult to cope with.

- Many of us are familiar with Edward de Bono's term 'lateral thinking' often described as 'thinking outside the box'. This is another skill that a bright dyslexic child will often use to amaze us if we give them the opportunity.

Visual, auditory, kinaesthetic – stronger together

Research has given us convincing proof that we have three dominant ways of absorbing experiences and learning from them:

visual (taking information in through our eyes),

auditory (taking information in through our ears),

kinaesthetic (taking information in through our bodies).

Each of us uses all three ways of learning, but each of us also has a preferred learning style. The most powerful learning comes when we combine two or more of the styles and when teachers or early years practitioners use all three sorts of stimuli and a range of teaching styles.

Children who are predominantly kinaesthetic learners (particularly if they also have more physical intelligence) are thought to be most likely to lose out in the education system. They may be labelled as hyperactive or be assumed to have a learning disorder when in fact they are craving to meet the desire to learn using their strongest intelligence. Little wonder then that they grow up thinking that they are not very clever. Schools have long recognised the challenge of helping children to reach their full potential while meeting the demands of the National Curriculum. The needs of a child with dyslexia, and others with specific learning difficulties, can stretch that challenge to its limits.

Practitioners and other professionals who work in the EYFS are in a unique and privileged position. They can begin to lay firm foundations for future learning and development, taking into account the different learning styles of each of the children in their care.

Knowing ourselves and the children

We can all be effective learners if we know how to identify and use our preferred learning style and our full range of intelligences. It is interesting that in some families the same intelligences are in evidence but in others, siblings excel in different intelligences. These differences should all be celebrated, but in some families and in society as a whole, some intelligences are more highly valued than others. We often admire a footballer for his skill on the pitch, or a singer for her sense of rhythm and drama, then we ask them to talk on a chat show and mock their lack of linguistic skill!

Some people think that the time of major breakthroughs in learning is past, and that the intelligence needed in the 21st Century is the ability to combine existing knowledge into new ways of approaching the challenges of our planet. It is interesting that famous figures such as Winston Churchill and Richard Branson were not particularly successful at academic education but have been hugely successful at changing perceptions about how to achieve. Albert Einstein was a dreamer and struggled with mathematics at school but went on to become the greatest scientist of his age. It will be fascinating to see how history views the achievements of Bob Geldolf and others who question our thinking and our attitudes.

Informal learning is natural and successful, and it is what pre-school children do best. They ask lots of questions, experiment with different approaches and ideas, get other people's reactions, watch others and practise for themselves and, most importantly, enjoy learning and are encouraged and praised when they succeed. Sadly, as children begin formal schooling things can go wrong. Learning through more formal methods can restrict the ability of children to use all the skills they have developed, and at worst, makes learners believe that there is only one way to learn.

Fortunately, recent thinking is influencing methods and a more integrated and active curriculum is being adopted by many schools.

Starring dyslexia!

These people (and many more) have overcome the problems of dyslexia to become successful in their chosen career.

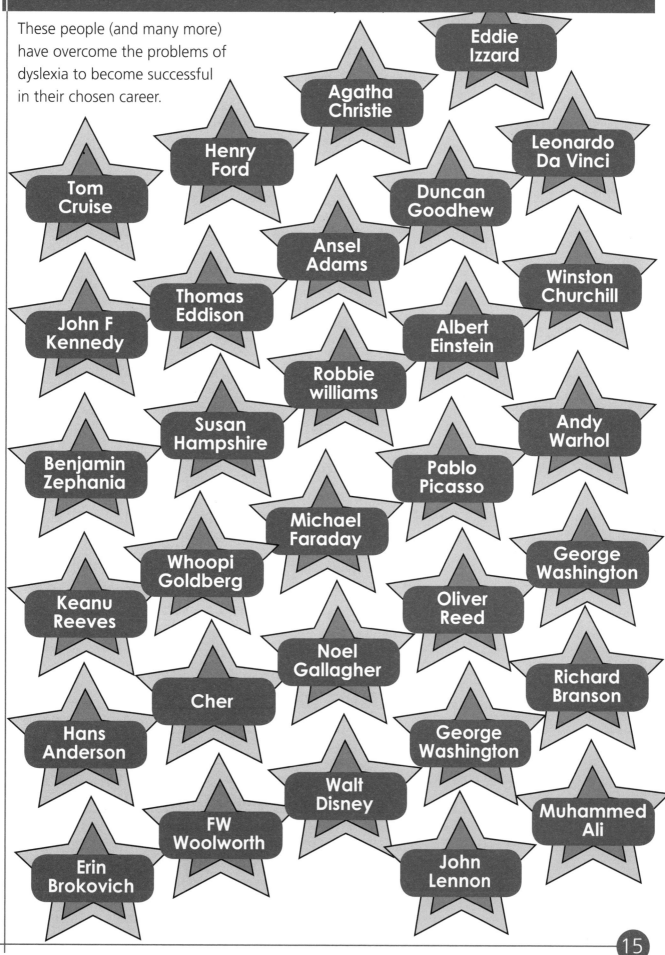

Eddie Izzard

Agatha Christie

Leonardo Da Vinci

Henry Ford

Duncan Goodhew

Tom Cruise

Ansel Adams

Winston Churchill

Thomas Eddison

Albert Einstein

John F Kennedy

Robbie williams

Susan Hampshire

Andy Warhol

Benjamin Zephania

Pablo Picasso

Michael Faraday

George Washington

Whoopi Goldberg

Keanu Reeves

Oliver Reed

Noel Gallagher

Richard Branson

Cher

Hans Anderson

George Washington

Walt Disney

FW Woolworth

Muhammed Ali

Erin Brokovich

John Lennon

How does it feel to have dyslexia?

Some reflections about early difficulties from adults with dyslexia

Many books have been written by people with dyslexia about their experiences when they were young, some of them make disturbing reading, but many are about overcoming difficulties in school to become successful and achieving adults. Famous people with dyslexia are in the public eye because of their exceptional skills in fields such as the media, the arts, sport, sciences, mathematics and architecture. So if a child is diagnosed as having dyslexia, or displays the characteristics of someone with specific learning difficulties, then it does not mean they will not succeed.

As with all effective early intervention, the way to success is often to work together to find out what the children are good at and to celebrate that, while finding ways to help them to cope with the problem areas.

Of course, a child with dyslexia will experience problems with reading and writing, that is what dyslexia is – a dysfunction with the lexicon (the written word), resulting in difficulties when you ask them to repeat the sound of a letter, to copy it onto paper or even to match it to another plastic letter which is exactly the same in every way. Success, praise and recognition of their individual strengths often gives children the courage to persevere with the difficult bits.

Problems for children with dyslexia are not confined to learning and development. Some children who have dyslexia are very capable, but problems with lack of co-ordination (many people with dyslexia are left handed) or struggling to pronounce certain words can get in the way. This can lead to teasing by other children, lack of understanding from adults, and understandable frustration and anger from the child. Sometimes the child's anger and frustration is misunderstood by others, who come to the conclusion that they have emotional and behavioural difficulties, when the real difficulty is with reading and writing.

You can see why it is so important for adults to observe, record and analyse children's strengths and weaknesses accurately and provide regular, timely help that will really make a difference. This is where parents can and should be directly involved in activities at home. A lively, interesting reading scheme which is appropriately structured and has lots of repetition at the right pace for the learner gives good practice for most young children. The regularity and repetition is particularly helpful for many children who show early signs of dyslexia or are learning slowly for some other reason.

Adults with dyslexia often tell how their parents and teachers were disappointed with them when they started school, thinking that they were being lazy or just not concentrating. There is also plenty of evidence that some children go to great lengthsto hide their difficulties. This behaviour can include anything from becoming the class clown, to being very busy doing very little, to feeling so anxious about going to school that real or imaginary illnesses persuade their parents or carers to keep them at home. Usually the behaviour is a real cry for help – all these children want is to be the same as everyone else.

Psychologists and other specialists can often help practitioners and parents to work out why a child is behaving in a particular way. Their experience is often just the thing to help the child and family to feel less anxious, and they can usually suggest ways to help the child to overcome their difficulties and do much better at school, some even going on to become high achievers. Many children with dyslexia go to university and do well, sometimes with very little extra support from their tutors. However, early disappointment in school can sadly stay with some people all their lives.

Adults with dyslexia often say how, when they are thinking about something, they see things in pictures rather than words like some other people. This can be a real skill leading them to be able to do things like visualising their way between home and school really well. Computers now are able to help the rest of us to see things in a similar way.

Some children have difficulty remember what is going to happen next. A pictorial timetable can help, both at home and in early years settings. It can also be a good idea to give children a little slip of paper to carry in their pocket to remind them of something. For a child who forgets what they went upstairs for, a picture can be a good reminder. When a child is able to begin to dress themselves, parents often find it helpful to put clothes on a chair in the right order and shoes side by side.

If we can help children to say 'I can't do that, I need some help', without feeling embarrassed, and help them to get really good at the things they do best, children will be more relaxed, and relaxed children are more successful.

Tip

Build in relaxation time for children with dyslexia – trying to concentrate in a noisy and busy environment can be very tiring

Inclusive practice – good for everyone

Inclusion is about creating a secure, accepting and stimulating atmosphere in which everyone, children and adults, are valued. In an inclusive setting people say they feel valued, at ease, content, happy and useful.

Inclusion works best in an effective learning environment:

- **Clear and appropriate learning objectives** – children thrive when they are set suitable learning challenges that meet their current strengths and stage of development.

- **Appropriate learning and teaching styles** – we need to be aware of and respond to children's diverse needs.

- **Access to resources and curriculum experiences** – if children are going to make progress we need to be able to assess and identify potential barriers to learning so that they can be helped to overcome them. These barriers could be learning based or related to health or social issues.

Three key factors underpin successful inclusion:

- **Positive attitudes** – having high expectations of all children, helping all children to participate, modelling and developing 'can do' attitudes in them.

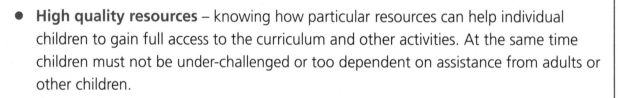

- **Relevant skills** – these can be gained through training, observing effective and experienced colleagues, and asking for support when needed.

- **High quality resources** – knowing how particular resources can help individual children to gain full access to the curriculum and other activities. At the same time children must not be under-challenged or too dependent on assistance from adults or other children.

The Disability Discrimination Act of 1995 made it '..unlawful for schools to discriminate against disabled pupils for a reason relating to their disability, without justification'. This applies to all public buildings, not just schools and it is law that schools must make 'reasonable adjustments' to accommodate the needs of children (and their parents or carers) who have special educational needs.

In order to help all children to learn:

- The task should be at the right level.

- The adults working with the child should work at the right pace, showing sensitivity to their needs.

- Practitioners need to be aware of individual children's abilities, motivation and physical and emotional well-being.

- The learning space needs to fit the purpose, and be well organised.

- The match of tasks and activities to the child's ability must be good – if a child consistently fails to achieve they can be put off learning, and if tasks are too easy they may become bored and fail to make the progress expected.

Good early years practice can help children to feel valued and included despite their special educational needs, showing all children that it is important to celebrate and accept difference and enjoy being part of a community.

Early indications of dyslexia

The usual pattern for children with dyslexia is for their diagnosis to take place at school. However, during the time before diagnosis, children can experience an increasing sense of frustration and failure. This can lead to lack of confidence, poor self-esteem and even behaviour difficulties. Parents and practitioners alike can feel equally frustrated with the child who appears to be 'as bright as a button' but who has difficulty with some aspects of communication, memory, coordination and concentration.

As professionals working with children in the EYFS, early years practitioners are in a unique position. They can observe all aspects of children's development and learning in an objective, professional way.

Awareness and understanding of the early signs of dyslexia, and knowledge of strategies to support children, will help to:

- alleviate frustration;
- improve self-confidence;
- foster positive feelings of achievement and success;
- support attention and concentration;
- improve communication and language skills;
- support partnership with parents.

Practitioners can achieve this by:

- observing the child at different times of the day, during child initiated and adult led play and other learning opportunities;
- gathering information and consulting with colleagues and parents or carers such as grandparents, childminders and other early years settings that the child attends;
- anticipating possible situations where difficulties might arise;
- careful planning, ensuring all practitioners in the setting are ready to offer just the right amount of support;
- breaking tasks down into small, achievable steps.

How to help

Observe
Collect information
Plan flexibly
Use a 'small steps' approach

It is important to remember that children who experience some of the difficulties associated with dyslexia, do not necessarily have dyslexia. There may be other reasons for their difficulties, such as:

- immaturity;

- a history of medical difficulties, leading to uneven development;

- speech and language delay or disorder;

- difficulty with attention and concentration, sometimes associated with other disorders such as ADD or ADHD;

- separation anxiety – the child who experiences distress and worry when separated from their parent or main carer;

- attachment disorders, when the typical pattern of infant/parent bonding has been disrupted;

- visual or hearing impairment;

- social and emotional difficulties at home;

- recent loss or trauma.

Children are unlikely to experience all of these, but several may be present in combination in children with or without dyslexia. However, we do know that early identification of individual difficulties is crucial, and early intervention of the right kind is even more important. (Code of Practice, DFES 2002). Children are at their most receptive during the early years, learning and growing at a phenomenal rate, and practitioners are often vital in providing support to children who may later receive a diagnosis of dyslexia. See also the early support materials at: **www.earlysupport.org.uk**

What to look for in children who may have dyslexia - the positive characteristics.

Children with early signs of dyslexia are often:

- artistic and creative with a strong imagination;

- good at construction and technical toys such as Lego;

- quick thinking, articulate and curious;

- interested in the environment;

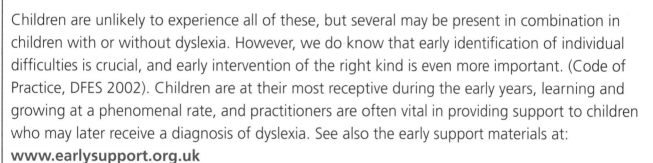

- eager to embrace new ideas and concepts;

- good at getting the 'gist' of things;

- quick to grasp new concepts;

- surprisingly mature for their age;

- able to figure things out, solve problems and work out puzzles;

- good at comprehension of stories read or told, and with a wide vocabulary.

However, some children may also display difficulties affecting their behaviour or learning. These may include:

- high **distractibility** and poor concentration;

- **inconsistent development**, for example, they may be good at some things but have surprising difficulty with others, leading to an uneven profile of development;

- **poor gross and fine motor coordination;**

- **'good' and 'bad' days** for no apparent reason;

- **poor short term memory** or self-organisation skills;

- **low self-esteem;**

- **difficulty with sequencing** – for example, may repeatedly attempt to put on clothes in the wrong order.

Key things to remember

- A child who is later diagnosed with dyslexia will not display all these early signs.

- Hearing and sight tests should always be undertaken to exclude any other possible causes.

- A child who does display some or most of these signs will not necessarily have dyslexia. Many children, at some stage, will show some of these areas of difficulty and they will usually disappear with maturity. Look for unexpected problems compared with the child's potential and proven abilities in other areas; a child with dyslexia will have marked and persistent difficulties in several areas.

- As with all children, the best approach is to adopt a 'can do' ethos in your setting, building on strengths and using small, achievable steps, to underpin all learning opportunities.

- Listen to the child's parents. Parents are very perceptive about their child and any concerns that they have must be taken seriously.

- A relationship of trust and mutual understanding between yourself and a child's parents is one of the most positive contributions you can make towards a child's development and learning.

- No two children with dyslexia are exactly alike.

Dyslexia and the Early Years Foundation Stage

Personal, social and emotional development

Some aspects of Personal, social and emotional development that may be observed in children who are showing early signs of uneven and/or delayed development are:

- over-reliance on adult help for aspects of personal care, such as dressing and undressing, using the toilet, eating;
- difficulties in remembering the routine of the session or day;
- low self-esteem resulting from failure to communicate or to complete tasks in the same way as other children;
- lack of confidence;
- poor disposition for learning;
- lack of persistence and concentration;
- difficulty making friends with other children;
- behaviour difficulties.

Any of the above may mean that children have problems with aspects and activities in the daily routine of an early years setting. For example:

- circle time
- story time
- imaginative play
- answering queries
- listening to new stories
- responding to verbal instructions
- group role play

Useful strategies include:

- Support children by giving encouragement and showing them how to co-operate, share and play with other children i.e. be good role models.
- Create opportunities for children to work and play alone and in groups of different sizes.
- Give help only when it is needed.
- Allow children to develop their own interests.
- Display positive images of others and be pro-active in your attitude to embracing and valuing differences.
- Plan for the development of independence skills, particularly for children who need more help.
- Use a structured, small steps approach to all learning opportunities.
- Ensure that each child has a 'Key Person', to provide continuity and promote emotional wellbeing.
- The Key Person must show that they value the child by being an active listener and an excellent role model.
- Have a clear structure and routine to the day.
- Give real responsibilities to children, such as planning the environment, serving snacks or taking messages.

- Foster feelings of self confidence and competence by ensuring that activities are enjoyable and giving children real choices.
- Allow children to choose their own challenges and solve their own problems.

'All children need achievable challenges so that they have positive experiences and learn to regard themselves as capable and successful.' (CGFS, 2000)

Support through specific programmes and resources

Other ways to support and develop Personal, social and emotional development include the use of specific sorts of programmes, resources and activities such as Circle Time and Persona Dolls.

Circle Time

Circle Time does not just mean sitting in a circle for different activities.It is a very specific approach, and needs careful planning to beeffective, but it is well worth the time and effort. The CircleTime approach can help children to gain confidence and self-esteem, it fosters good listening, concentration and cooperation skills. If you have enough staff, it is best to work with small groups of children to start with. The youngest children need not sit in a circle to start with, but you can gradually encourage this. Take time at the very beginning to establish the format and organisation of your Circle Time as these skills, once learned, will support children in all their future learning.

Children who are experiencing difficulties, may need extra support; this needs to be anticipated and planned for before starting on the programme. This could mean shorter sessions and a really interesting and lively content. Some children may need to be observers from the edge of the group, or even from another part of the room. If you make Circle Time lively and fun, children will respond positively and will really look forward to it.

Persona Dolls

This is another approach that can be used to support children's confidence and self-esteem. It is extremely useful in enabling children to explore difficult issues in a sensitive and non-threatening way. The skilled practitioner, using a Persona Doll, can begin to address all sorts of issues such as bullying, sadness and anxiety. It is also a wonderful medium for exploring diversity and different kinds of achievement.

Storysacks, puppets, creative activities and role play can also make significant contributions to children's development.

Health Warning

Proper training in the correct use of Persona Dolls and Circle Time are really important to make this approach successful.

Emotional Literacy

There has been much interest recently about Emotional Intelligence and Emotional Literacy (see page 11). Put very simply, Emotional Literacy emphasises the importance of children beginning to learn to recognise how they are feeling and how to express those feelings in an appropriate and acceptable way. This could involve:

- adults talking about feelings and modelling their reactions;
- children and adults talking about emotions using books, stories, songs, role play and Persona Dolls.

Only when children begin to recognise their own feelings, and begin to learn how to name them, can they begin to be aware of the feelings of others. This area of emotional development is particularly important when supporting children with problems of self confidence and feelings of self-worth.

Communication, language and literacy

All children begin to learn how to communicate and use language from the moment they are born. Learning will take place at different rates depending on a huge variety of factors. The role of the practitioner is to observe how children communicate and how they use language to express themselves and interact with others.

There are several key aspects of language development that can cause difficulties for children, who may or may not be diagnosed later with dyslexia, and if these difficulties are observed in any child, steps should be taken to provide additional support. In the EYFS Framework this area of the curriculum is described as being at the heart of young children's learning. The practical guidance, cards and disk contains a wealth of materials for advice and information.

A child under five may:

- be unable to remember two or more instructions in sequence;
- confuse names of objects;
- use 'Spoonerisms' such as 'par cark';
- have difficulty remembering nursery rhymes;
- have difficulty clapping or moving to a rhythm;
- be unable to associate sounds with words;
- mix up sounds in words of more than one syllable e.g. aminal for animal;
- use substitute words e.g. lampshade for lamppost;
- be easily distracted, with poor attention and concentration;
- be confused with directional words such as up and down; or with prepositions such as over and under;
- not recognise their own name, for instance on their coat peg.

A child under five may not:

- have learnt the alphabet, or the sounds represented by letters;
- have learnt to read, apart from a few simple words;
- be able to hold a pencil correctly;
- remember sequences.

Supporting Children's Language Development

These ideas will help children to develop communication skills and their use of language for thinking. The emphasis is on:

- **sharing stories**
- **using rhymes**
- **playing listening games**
- **encouraging memory**

These activities will support all children with early literacy, but will be especially helpful for children experiencing difficulties. There are many activities that will help children to develop their fine motor skills in readiness for mastering the art of writing. For a more comprehensive list of ideas, see Appendicies on page 41.

Key techniques to remember are to:

- **Talk naturally** to children;

- **Give a running commentary** on what you are doing, using simplified language if necessary, to match the child's level of understanding;

- **Comment on what you are doing**, to reinforce words such as on/off, over/under, up/down. (These directional and positional words are very important as children who may have dyslexia are likely to find them particularly difficult to master.);

- **Comment on a child's play/activity**, using language that matches the child's understanding. (This is a very powerful way to encourage communication. Without directing the child's play or taking control, you are showing that you really value what the child is doing. You are also reinforcing vocabulary and sowing the seeds of language for thinking.);

- **Play listening games**, using environmental sounds, transport and animal sounds, identifying and matching sounds, recorded voices, stop/go games when the music starts and stops, and other listening and responding games, guessing the sound of the object in a container. Play with variations in voice levels, whisper simple statements or instructions;

- **Play turn taking games** that involve cooperation and interaction. Keep them simple and one-to-one to start with, involving other children once the basics have been learned. For example - take turns rolling a ball to each other, putting pieces in a puzzle, adding bricks to a tower or a model, turning the pages in a book;

- **Have fun with nursery rhymes**, using lots of repetition, and encouraging the child to join in with the last word of a rhyme. Substitute words, and make up your own rhymes;

- **Use songs and rhymes involving memory and sequencing**. Play 'pairs' and picture matching games, 'Simon Says', or remembering objects in sequence. (These activities can all start off very simply and gradually become more difficult to suit the needs of the individual child. Similarly, all can be played with a group of children. The older or more capable children can help, by holding the book, giving instructions, or managing the 'props'.);

- **Enjoy stories together**, simplifying language to match the child's understanding. Repeat favourite stories and encourage the child to join in with the repetitive phrases. Children always love this. Get cosy, make it exciting with lots of anticipation for 'lift the flap' or 'pull the tab' books. Spend time just looking at the pictures and talk about what is happening;

- **Talk about stories and incidents afterwards** or at other times. Simplify this if necessary, so that you are talking about single events, and gradually increase the sequence e.g. 'Do you remember, we played outside?' is more useful if increased to - 'Do you remember, we went outside, and we played football?'

- **Emphasise the rhythm of words and rhymes**. Try breaking up the syllables to a beat, starting with 'one' beat and gradually increasing;

- **Dance and move about!** This will help with rhythm and whole body movements. If the child has difficulty, stress the beat by clapping and stamping. Try to incorporate large movements where the arms cross over the mid line.
Remember to praise any efforts made;

- **Always give instructions in small steps**, rather than a long sequence.

Problem solving, reasoning and numeracy

A rich mathematical environment surrounds children in early years settings. This includes displays, counting, songs, rhymes, stories, birthdays, toys, equipment, shapes, language, measures, and much more.

Some children with dyslexia may have:

- poor concentration and easily distracted;

- poor gross and fine motor co-ordination;

- good and bad days for no apparent reason;

- poor short term memory and difficulties with self organisation skills;

- low self-esteem;

- difficulty with sequences in a general sense, and abstract terms.

Key things to remember:

- **encourage children to talk** about what they are doing/have done and to listen to each other;

- **model language** by describing what children are doing as you work/play alongside them e.g. 'You made the car go straight ahead and then turn left';

- **value** children's own spontaneous language, e.g. 'My shape has three pointy bits';

- extend what children have said in different words, e.g. 'Yes, it's got three corners';

- **set up activities** which encourage children to describe and explain, e.g. 'Say what you can feel in the feely bag';

- **encourage children to compare**, e.g. 'How are these two shapes different?';

- **use real examples** and everyday objects and equipment.

All children in the Early Years Foundation Stage enjoy real play opportunities. The best way to help children learn new ideas and concepts is to provide lots of stimulating and interesting materials and hands-on experience. Daily contact with a range of tactile and physical experiences gives enormous pleasure, and helps learning, particularly for those children who are experiencing some of the early signs of dyslexia, such as poor memory or difficulties with language. Integrating or combining the use of the senses in this kind of play helps cognitive and language development.

Children who are later diagnosed as having dyslexia will have gained appropriate support through this multi-sensory approach which they can use throughout their school lives and beyond.

Some examples of materials and activities ideal for multi-sensory play are are:

- Playdough with different textures, colours and smells.

- Water, in trays, bowls, buckets, from taps, indoors and out.

- Foam, gloop, cooked pasta and other malleable materials.

- Wet and dry sand, in big trays with big equipment; in small trays with tiny equipment.

- Painting with hands, feet, and bodies on different surfaces indoors and out.

- Cooking, snack making and other food activities.

- Using feet and hands in different materials, e.g. jelly, pasta and on different surfaces: carpet, wood, sand, concrete, grass.

As early years practitioners, you will be able to think of many more examples.

Remember the golden rules:

- **Break tasks down into small steps;**

- **Allow time for practice;**

- **Use lots of repetition;**

- **Build on what children know already**

- **Give prompts and appropriate rewards.**

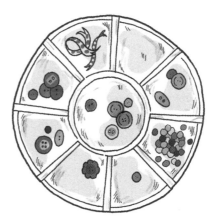

Try to:

- Talk about numbers in everyday life;

- Talk about and encourage comparing and combining numbers;

- Give practical opportunities for sharing and grouping;

- Allow children to experience the properties of shapes, 2D and 3D;

- Enable children to experiment with the properties of shape and space;

- Offer lots of opportunity to pack, fill, empty and to 'make things fit';

- Talk about the routine of the day, the sequence of events. (Particularly important for children who have problems with sequencing);

- Show an interest in how children arrive at solutions, e.g. 'tell me how you made you model'.

Final key points to remember:

- **Use all the strategies outlined in the Areas of Learning, particularly in 'Communication, Language and Literacy' and 'Personal, Social and Emotional Development'.**

- **Children do not learn in separate compartments.**

- **Communication and language are at the heart of all interactions with children, their parents and our colleagues.**

Knowledge and understanding of the world

This area of learning can be very exciting for all children. It involves a wide range of stimulating and focused practical activities, based on everyday situations and experiences, as well as more challenging and unusual experiences.

Provide daily opportunities with everyday objects to explore their surroundings:

- children can learn how to use a range of tools such as computers, magnifiers, gardening tools, scissors, hole punches and screwdrivers;

- encounters with creatures, people, plants and objects in their natural environments and in real life situations provide lots of opportunities for children to engage with the world in a very practical and concrete way;

- there are opportunities to solve problems for example using pulleys to raise heavy objects or observing the effect of increasing the incline of a slope on how fast a vehicle travels;

- this area of learning provides a wealth of opportunity for practitioners to encourage and support children in their risk taking and problem solving. This is also an opportunity to promote self-esteem and confidence;

Strategies to develop communication skills will be just as relevant to this and all other areas of learning. They include the advice to:

- **Talk naturally** with children.

- **Give a running commentary** on what you are doing, using simplified language if necessary, to match the child's level of understanding.

- **Comment on what you are doing**, to reinforce words such as on/off, over/under, up/down. (These directional or positional words are very important as children who have dyslexia are likely to find them particularly difficult to understand).

- **Comment on a child's play/activity**. Use language to match the child's understanding. (This is a very powerful way to encourage communication. Without directing the child's play or taking control, you are showing that you really value what the child is doing. You are also reinforcing vocabulary and sowing the seeds of language for thinking).

- **Play listening games**, using environmental sounds, transport and animal sounds, identifying and matching sounds, recorded voices, stop/go games when the music starts and stops, and other listening and responding games, guessing the sound of the object in a container. Play with variations in voice levels, whisper simple statements or instructions. Always give instructions in small steps, rather than a long sequence.

The Early Learning Goals for exploration and investigation, require opportunities to encourage children to record their observations and findings using a range of different media. Making a tape or a model, or using video or photography, to record what they see and notice, will help them make connections and remember sequences. This will be particularly helpful for children experiencing the early signs of dyslexia.

Again, these activities will also be a great support for Communication, Language and Literacy. Children and adults with dyslexia are often great problem solvers. Children who display some of the early indications of dyslexia can excel in this area of learning. Practitioners can model investigative behaviour by using questions such as 'How might it work?'

Children may need help to remember what they have done and the tools and materials they have used to construct, shape, assemble and join materials. The use of video, digital photographs and/or simple pictures can provide really useful support.

Older children with dyslexia will often be best supported by the use of ICT equipment, and where better to begin familiarity with a wide variety of ICT equipment than in the Early Years? The Early Learning Goal for information and communication technology provides many opportunities for children to explore this area.

Physical development

Children who are experiencing problems associated with the early signs of dyslexia, may have a history of some of the following difficulties.

The child:

- walked early but did not crawl – was a 'bottom shuffler'or a 'wriggler';
- has poor co-ordination in some activities, but is good at manipulating things like Lego;
- is clumsy, with poor balance, bumping into things, falling over;
- is uncertain of which hand to use;
- has difficulty telling left from right;
- has difficulty dressing – puts clothes on in the wrong order, can't cope easily with buttons, zips etc.
- has difficulties with catching/kicking/throwing/hopping/skipping;
- has difficulty in clapping or moving to a rhythm.

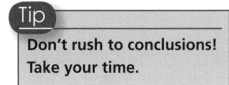

Tip

Don't rush to conclusions! Take your time.

Professionals, working with young children, all know that physical activity is crucial for young children's development and learning and some children find this more difficult than others. Sufficient space, equipment, access and time are all necessary for young children to develop all their physical skills. Children who experience any of the difficulties listed above, may need support during physical play. From organised games to individual interactions with adults, children will need time and support to develop their confidence, and fun and enjoyment are of course key to children's learning.

'Young children's physical development is inseparable from all other aspects of development because they learn through being active and interactive.' Curriculum Guidance for the Foundation Stage (DfES 2000)

'The physical development of babies and young children must be encouraged through the provision of opportunities for them to be active and interactive and to improve their skills of coordination, control, manipulation and movement (EYFS 2008)'.

Gross motor skills

Key things to remember:

- Large movements such as waving a flag, or 'painting' with large paint brushes and water, must be mastered and practised, before children can cope with smaller movements successfully.

- Gross motor play, including games where the children need to move in different directions in the outside play area, will help children to internalise concepts of direction, here are some examples:

  - run to the fence

  - run to the gate

  - walk backwards to your friend

  - go sideways like a crab.

- Cycling, on tricycles to start with, is an excellent way for children to improve their awareness of their body in space.
  Take care to ensure that the equipment is the right size, so the child is well balanced and can put their feet on the ground easily.

- Dancing will help children with their sense of rhythm and whole body movements. Stress the beat by clapping and stamping or banging a drum, encourage children to do the same.

Remember

Children with co-ordination difficulties need:

- more time to practise skills
- lots of repetition
- tasks and challenges to be broken down into small achievable steps

Fine motor skills

Activities that encourage gripping and fine manipulation of objects are essential in developing fine motor skills. Here are some ideas:

- Make pouring, filling and emptying interesting by using different materials such as pasta, rice, seeds, sand, sawdust.

- A variety of equipment will add interest - try funnels, jugs of different sizes, bottles, different sized spoons/ladles, turkey baster, tongs, tweezers, sponges.

There are hundreds of ways to encourage physical skills of all kinds. See Appendix 2 (pages 41-45) for more ideas of how to develop fine motor skills.

Creative development

Children who later may be diagnosed with dyslexia often have strong creative abilities, and this can provide an important opportunity for social interaction and establishing friendships. Creative work also gives wonderful opportunities to foster self esteem and a genuine pride in their own achievements. This is particularly important for children who are experiencing difficulties in other aspects of their development. If a child has particular strengths in this area you can really celebrate achievement, effort and motivation and thus give a huge boost to a child's self confidence and feelings of self worth.

By focusing on supporting children's creativity, practitioners will be helping them to make their own decisions, take risks, and play and experiment with ideas. It is important to achieve a balance between adult led activities and child initiated activities, taking care not to direct all the time. Creativity also helps children to make connections between different experiences and different environments, and to develop understanding of self and others. Creative development, as an area of learning, provides many opportunities for practitioners to explore the use of all the senses. A multi-sensory approach will be particularly relevant for those children who are experiencing early signs of dyslexia.

Art, music, dance, role play and imaginative play also contribute to achievement of goals acrsoss all areas of learning.

- a stimulating environment in which creativity, originality and expressiveness are valued;

- a wide range of activities that children can respond to by using many senses;

- sufficient time for children to explore, develop ideas and finish working at their ideas;

- opportunities for children to express their ideas through a wide range of types of representation;

- resources from a variety of cultures to stimulate different ways of thinking;

- opportunities to work alongside artists and other creative adults;

and

- accommodating children's specific religious or cultural beliefs relating to particular forms of art or methods of representation.

Working with others

Working with parents and carers

Remember:

- Parents are often very anxious if their child is having difficulties.

- Being a parent can be a complex and difficult role.

- Parents will be almost certainly be interested in the opportunity to tell you about their views – so listen carefully!

- Find ways in which parents can be involved in the planning process.

Create an atmosphere of shared responsibility, communicate and share knowledge by making some of the following part of your normal practice:

- Involve parents and carers before the child starts attending your setting.

- Offering a home visit before the child starts can make a big difference to the settling period of the child.

- When arranging individual meetings with the parent/carer, remember that these are sometimes difficult for parents during the work day or in the evening but they are invaluable, so make every effort to keep in regular contact.

- Home/early years/pre-school books provide an easy way of communicating with parents or carers. These could include photographs as well as writing.

- Inviting parents to join the group on a visit or trip is often a good way of getting to know the parent and gives the parent an opportunity to work alongside practitioners.

- Invite parents to lunch sessions. For some parents this is a good time if they are picking up or dropping children off at midday.

- Establish a regular parent group meeting. If these are held during the day child minding or babysitting will not be necessary.

- Weekly/monthly newsletters can explain what has been happening and events planned for the future.

Remember: If parents do not choose to become involved, ensure that they are given regular sensitive feedback on their child's progress.

If a child is having difficulties:

- Contact the parents as soon as possible.

- Enlist their support.

- Meet with the SENCO and discuss possible 'early years action'. See **www.earlysupport.org.uk**

- Focus on the positive. Send home good messages about times when the child has been successful.

- Focus on working together to solve any problems. Suggest ways in which difficulties can be resolved by being consistent in an approach. Work on a plan together.

- Plan a follow up. Arrange another meeting to review how things are going.

Exploring family history

Dyslexia can be inherited, so it may be appropriate to discuss not only the child's history, but also to try sensitivity to find out about difficulties any of the other members of the family may have had when trying to acquire new skills.

Special Educational Needs (SEN) Code of Practice

The SEN Code of Practice provides advice to all Local Authorities, early years settings and others on how to carry out their statutory duties for making provision for children's special educational needs. All early years settings **must** take into account the guidance in the **SEN Code of Practice (DfES, 2001)**.

They must tell the parent and Local Authority when any extra or different help is given to a child. This might be some form of extra adult help, a different way of teaching things or the use of special equipment. In early education settings this help is called **Early Years Action**. **An Individual Education Plan (IEP)** will need to be written for the child (see an example at the end of the book). Two or three targets are agreed between parents and practitioners, and these must be broken down into small steps. **Chapter 2 of the SEN Code of Practice** (p16-26) is all about working in partnership with parents.

Ways to help at home

Suggestions for the parent or carer helping a child at home

If a child shows any of the early general indications of having dyslexia, the following activities could be suggested for parents/carers to support their child at home. Suggest adults use as many of the senses as possible during activities.

Sense of sight:

- Look at all of the colours of fruit and vegetables in the supermarket or in a vegetable rack.

- Watch water go down the plug hole and using appropriate language to describe what you see.

- Watch the leaves/trees/flowers blowing in the wind, and describe them.

- Share picture books, comics, children's magazines and DVDs.

- Let them feel a kite pulling on its string, push a car along the floor.

- Look at paintings and drawings in books or visit the real thing!

- Go on walks and point out things as you go. Take photos so you can recall what you did and saw.

Sense of touch:

- Making and playing with playdough, tracing shapes in things like cornflour, soil, wet and dry sand.

- Water play in the bath or sink, handling different shaped objects.

- Finger games, songs and rhymes.

- Handling books of different shapes and sizes with different types of pages and covers such as flap books.

- Use plastic or card letters and numbers to handle and talk about.

- Hide things in a bag and get the child to guess by touch what it is before they see it.

- Encourage them to touch things with different textures.

- Join them in doing puzzles at the appropriate level.

Who's who in multi-agency working?

This covers everyone working with children, young people and families working together. Anyone working in the early years will at some time need to liaise with the following groups of people.

Speech and language therapists are often based at a local health clinic and will do visits at home or at Early Year's settings to support children with speech and language difficulties. They sometimes work with an individual or in small groups to develop the child's communication and language skills.

Physiotherapists and Occupational therapists help to support children's physical development. They may provide exercises for the child to do regularly to support their motor skills.

Educational psychologists work alongside schools, settings and Local Authorities and offer advice and support to any school setting. There is often one EP who specialises in the Early Years. They assess the learning needs of the children.

Early Years Foundation Stage advisory teachers provide specialist pre-school support for the development of skills for learning alongside other pre-school workers, specialist teachers and portage workers.

Health Visitors provide parents with advice and support on the health of their child.

You may also meet:

Early Years practitioners: setting managers, key workers, a range of different practitioners and the special needs co-ordinator (SENCO) who ensures the child has the best possible support from the team and an Individual Education or Learning Plan (IEP).

and of course there will be:

Social Services professionals, HomeStart volunteers and occupational therapists. The team may also include Parent Partnership workers providing independent parental support. In addition, parents may receive advice and support from local or national voluntary organisations.

Books, resources and websites

Frames of Mind: Theories of Multiple Intelligences
Howard Gardner
Fontana Press

Emotional Intelligence
Daniel Goleman
Bantam Books

www.listening-books.org.uk
This site will lend listening books – early years settings can subscribe.

www.persona-doll-training.org
for Persona dolls, training and resources.

Action Raps
Ros Bayley
Lawrence Educational Publication
ISBN: 1-903670-42-X

The Little Book of Persona Dolls
and
The Little Book of Circle Time
Featherstone Education Ltd

Circle Time for the Very Young
Margaret Collins
Lucky-Duck Publishers
ISBN: 1-873942-53-2

Combating Discrimination: Persona Dolls in Action
Babette Brown
Trentham Books

The Early Years Foundation Stage (May 2008)
DCFS Publications
Tel: 0845 6022260 Ref.no. 00261-2008 PCK-EN

Dyslexia in The Early Years: A Practical Guide to Teaching and Learning
Dimitra Hartas
Routledge publishers – Taylor & Francis Group

Here We Go Round
Jenny Moseley & Helen Sonnet
Positive Press
ISBN: 0 953012212

How to Develop Numeracy in Children with Dyslexia
Pauline Clayton
Learning Development Agency (LDA)

Playing with sounds: a supplement to Progression in Phonics
DfES Publications
Ref. no: 0280-2004
This file contains lots of activities to help support the early development of listening skills and understanding phonics. The cards 2-7 are particularly useful for the early years.

Sense Toys: Early Movement Skills
Naomi Benari
Speechmark publications
Special Educational Needs: Code of Practice
DfES 2001
Ref.no: DfES 581/2001

Thinking Child; and **Thinking Child Resource Book**
Nicola Call with Sally Featherstone
Network Continuum

L is for Sheep; Getting Ready for Phonics
Ed: Sally Featherstone
Featherstone Education Ltd
a range of nationally recognised early years experts guide pratitioners through the maze of advice on teaching phonics.

British Dyslexia Association
98 London Road
Reading
RG1 5AU
Helpline:01189668271
www.bda-dyslexia.org

Dyslexia Action
Head Office and National Training and
Resources Centre
Park House
Wick Road
Egham
Surrey TW20 0HH
Tel: 01784 222 300
www.dyslexiaaction.org.uk

www.dyslexiahelp.co.uk
This site gives information, has links to
other sites and is particularly useful for
parents.

www.pre-school.org.uk
This pre-school Learning Alliance is an
educational charity specialising in early
years. It gives information and advice, is
involved with research and training and
provides support for early years settings.

www.ndna.org.uk
National Day Nurseries Association is a
national charity which aims to enhance
the development and education of children
in the early years, through the provision
of support services to members.

www.ncma.org.uk
The National Childminding Association works
with registered childminders and nannies,
as well as other individuals and organisation.

Early Support
www.earlysupport.org.uk

Early Support is the government programme
to achieve better co-ordinated, family focused
services for young disabled children and
their families.

101 ways to develop fine motor skills

'Fiddly Things for Little Fingers', 101 ways to develop fine motor skills
Collected by Caroline Davies and Michelle Tapper: Advisory Teachers for Poole LA

- Pour large beans or pasta from jug to jug

- Pour rice or seeds from jug to jug

- Pour rice or seeds from a jug into two or more containers of different sizes

- Pour rice or seeds from a jug into a plastic jar with a lid

- Pour water or sand from jug to jug

- Pour water or sand into two containers of different sizes

- Pour water or sand from a jug to a bottle using a funnel

- Pour water or sand from bottle to bottle using a funnel

- Pour water or sand from a jug into three different containers

- Pour water or sand into three different containers using a funnel

- Make patterns with felt shapes, wooden or glass beads, or shells

- Create a collage using seeds, beans or leaves

- Transfer lentils, dried peas or butter beans between two bowls using a spoon (vary the size of the spoon)

- Transfer rice or seeds between two egg cups using a spoon

- Transfer rice or seeds between two small identical bowls using a spoon

- Transfer rice or seeds between the sections of an egg box, with a spoon

- Transfer water between two identical containers using a sponge

- Transfer water between two identical containers using a turkey baster

- Transfer water between two small identical containers using a pipette

- Transfer water onto a soap mat using a pipette

- Transfer marbles or pasta between two identical containers with tongs

- Transfer lentils or seeds between two identical containers or saucers with tweezers

- Transfer lentils or seeds onto a soap mat with tweezers

- Transfer lentils or seeds into a small box with tweezers

- Transfer seeds between small yogurt pots with tweezers

- Transfer objects - marbles, plastic spiders or pasta with tongs or tweezers into a sorting tray

- Transfer seeds or black beans between two identical saucers using scissors or tweezers

- Transfer 'spongy glitter balls' between two cups

- Transfer coloured beads into correct coloured sections in a basket

- Transfer stamps with tweezers

- Transfer haricot beans onto a soap pad

- Transfer 'plastic eggs' into an egg box using tongs

- Open and close interesting empty plastic bottles

- Open and close interesting boxes, for example unusual shaped boxes and lids (try KEA for cheap boxes)

- Open and close interesting purses with treasure inside

- Open and close nuts and bolts

- Open and close drawstring bags

- Open and close padlocks and combination locks

- Use a dustpan and brush for sweeping

- Use a magnet to pick up a variety of objects

- Attach pegs of different sizes onto a plastic flower pot

- Peg a pair of shoes or wellies together

- Brush a doll's hair or a pony's tail

- Thread beads, pasta tubes or cotton reels onto a string or ribbon

- Weave with paper strips or ribbon through net

- Place beads into three or four screw top plastic jars or film canisters

- Use large chalks and salt, put salt into a pestle and mortar; grind with pestle; add chalk and grind some more; salt changes colour; pour into plastic jars and use to paint with

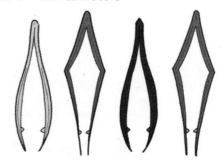

- Dress themselves

- Sort shells by colour or size

- Cut fruit and vegetables

- Peg objects onto a washing line using different sized pegs

- Spread butter on toast

- Manipulate materials (playdough, cooking ingredients, plasticine, cornflour or sand mousse) by pinching, poking, kneading, squeezing and rolling

- Squeeze water out of a bottle

- Push objects for example, a soap dispenser or buttons on a till

- Investigate cooking ingredients - stir, whisk, knead or sieve. Use knives, forks, spoons and chopsticks

- Use biscuit cutters

- Squeeze materials, icing from an icing bag, glitter glue or toothpaste from a tube

- Practise brushing own teeth

- Sort gems into a partitioned box

- Hole punch small squares of paper to make a necklace

- Create a picture using tap-a-tap-shapes

- Snip strips of paper with scissors

- Sharpen a pencil

- Staple paper together

- Join paper together using treasury tags

- Attach materials together using split pins

- Fold paper to make a fan

- Tear newspaper

- Use large paper clips to join card or paper together

- Handle small world toys for example, farm set or Playmobil people

- Construct using small equipment for example, wooden bricks or Duplo

- Complete a sewing card

- Post a shape into a sorter or a letter into a post box

- Pop bubbles in bubble wrap

- Piece a jigsaw together

- Create a 'fuzzy felt' picture

- Turn pages in a book or magazine

- Use a screwdriver to take a toy train apart (and try and put it back together again!)

- Sprinkle seeds, sand or glitter

- Finger paint

- Trace pictures or shapes

- Wind up a clockwork toy or a ball of string (racing car game)

- Print and paint using a range of materials using different sized brushes, combs or cotton reels

- Play musical instruments by tapping, stroking or strumming

- Use ICT equipment, for example controlling a computer mouse or take photographs with a digital camera

- Use finger puppets or make shadow puppets

- Correctly hold a pencil or crayon

- Open 'Russian Dolls', sort and put back together

- Learn to handle real tools safely for example, a hacksaw, a spade or a hammer

- Use a glue spreader

- Wash and dry up

- Recite finger rhymes, for example Incy Wincy Spider

- Push buttons on a telephone

- Remove and replace pen lids

- Wrap a present using sellotape

- Unwrap a present

- Peel fruit - a banana or an orange

- Put a letter or note into an envelope

- Dress dolls or teddies, manipulate buttons, zips, laces etc

- Use tiny whisks and scoops in sand or gloop

Plan some of these activities for your setting and add some of your own ideas here.

Our ideas

_____

_____

_____

_____

_____

_____

_____

_____

_____

_____

_____

_____

_____

Individual Education Plan – EYFS

Name: .... dob: ....../....../......

Involved Adults: ....

Key Person:...

Date:....../....../...... E.Y.A. E.Y.A.+

S.A.

Strengths:	Preferred activities:	Areas for development:

NB Plans to be based in play using preferred learning styles and favourite activities.

Target 1:	Activities and resources	ELGs	Celebration of achievement:

Target 2:	Activities and resources	ELGs	Celebration of achievement:

Suggestions for support to be offered at home:

side 2 (Review process) overleaf

Review

1. Parent/carer comments:

2. Staff comments:

3. Additional comments/ and reports from people not present:

Signatures (as appropriate)

Parent/carer: ....

SENCO/Provider:...

Date for next review:......./......./.......

Other titles in this series

Including Children with:

Attention and Behaviour Difficulties (ABD)
by Maureen Garner

Autistic Spectrum Disorders (ASD)
by Clare Beswick

Down's Syndrome
by Clare Beswick

Asperger's Syndrome
by Clare Beswick

Working Within the P Levels
by Kay Holman and Janet Beckett

Developmental Co-ordination Disorder (Dyspraxia)
by Sharon Drew

Published 2009 by A&C Black Publishers Limited
36 Soho Square, London W1D 3QY
www.acblack.com

First published by Featherstone Education Limited, September 2006
October

ISBN 9781408120804

Text © Chris Chandler, Meryl Morton, Sheila Smith, 2006
Illustrations © Martha Hardy, 2006
Editor, Sally Featherstone

A CIP record for this publication is available from the British Library.
All rights reserved. No part of this publication may be reproduced
in any form or by any means - graphic, electronic, or mechanical, including
photocopying, recording, taping or information storage or retrieval systems -
without the prior permission in writing of the publishers.
Printed in Great Britain by Latimer Trend & Company Limited
This book is produced using paper that is made from wood grown in
managed, sustainable forests. It is natural, renewable and recyclable.
The logging and manufacturing processes conform to the environmental
regulations of the country of origin.

**To see our full range of titles
visit www.acblack.com**

Including Children with Early Signs of Dyslexia in the Early Years Foundation Stage

371.9144 CMA

**Wiltshire College
Salisbury Library
Southampton Road
Salisbury SP1 2LW
01722 344325**

Wiltshire College
Salisbury

- 2 DEC 2013

2 4 APR 2014

2 2 MAY 2014
- 2 DEC 2014

- 6 JAN 2015

- 6 JAN 2015

1 6 JUN 2015

0 2 NOV 2015

Items must be returned or renewed on or before the last
date stamped above.
Borrowers will be charged the replacement cost of any item
which is lost or damaged.

Chris Chandler, Mary ... Smith

Illustrated by
Martha Hardy

Wiltshire College

75884